Flight into Reality

Rowan Tree Ireland Press, Booterstown, Co. Dublin
ISBN 978 1 872224 00 8
Printed by Naas Printing, Co. Kildare

Naas Printing uses environmentally friendly products of managed forests

First published 1989

Illustrations and Artwork: Rosemarie Rowley

Also by Rosemarie Rowley:

Poetry

The Broken Pledge	Martello, Dublin, 1985
The Sea of Affliction	Rowan Tree Press, 1987, 2010
Politry	Rowan Tree Press, 1988
Hot Cinquefoil Star	Rowan Tree Press, 2002 inc. ***Flight into Reality, The Poet's Visit, The Puzzle Factory, A Ruby Garland for George and Nora, Letter to Kathleen Raine***
In Memory of Her	Rowan Tree Press, 2004, 2008 inc. ***Betrayal into Origin (Dancing & Revolution in the Sixties), The Wake of Wonder, Faustina in Sestinae***

Translations:

You Are the Earth from the Italian of Mimmo Morina,
Alma Tellus from the Italian of Mimmo Morina,
Euro Editions, 1996, 1997

WEBSITE: www.rosemarierowley.ie

FLIGHT INTO REALITY

ROSEMARIE ROWLEY

ROWAN TREE IRELAND PRESS

Praise for Rosemarie Rowley

Kathleen Raine on *Flight into Reality*

"What impressed me immediately is Rosemarie's use of terza rima, with sustained skill, at times with eloquence ... Here is an attempt to examine the experience, suffering and nature of women seriously, with honesty and humility. The argument of the poem, which uses the symbolic structure the myth of Isis and Osiris, is that balance and love between the sexes, difficult as it may be, is to be desired, and that the responsibility lies with women as well as men ... It is an impressive, passionate exploration of failures and renewed hope and faith ... Strange that it would seem strange to read a poem by a woman that brings love into the equation, and spiritual aspiration!"

"A master of form" – **Brendan Kennelly**
"100% improvement on Christina Rossetti" – **Geoffrey Thurley**
"Her voice is one of heart-breaking beauty" – **Roz Cowman**
"Originality, commitment, and real literary ability" – **Eiléan Ní Chuilleanáin**
"I like the poems. I keep hearing something in them that I'm always listening for ... and rarely catch" – **Ted Hughes**
"Her range of vocabulary and phrasing is impressive. a true poet ... her finest poems wear their learning lightly – she excels as a critic" – **Declan Kiberd**
"Lyrics of a rare strength and delicacy" – **John McGahern**
"I have listened to (***Flight into Reality***) with a lot of pleasure. I think it is quite beautiful and very thought-provoking – **Brendan Glacken**
"Startling" – **Nuala O Faoláin**

Dedicated to the memory of my best friend Georgina Beirnes (1942-1974) and to her husband Alex Burns and their children

CONTENTS

In the Egyptian legend, Isis was the sister of Osiris. The cult of Osiris was distinguished by the expenditure of powerful emotion. Initially, Osiris was a king who ruled over Egypt in an idyllic order. This was broken by Seth, his wicked brother, who dared Osiris to lie in a coffin. The chest was then thrown into the Nile. All sources agree that Seth tore up Osiris' body and scattered the pieces. Isis seeks her husband's body, who is her mystical brother, and eventually finds all the parts save one – the organ of generation – and with the help of her sister Nephytys puts him together again. She is unable to bring him fully back to life. There was in Egypt, surrounded by desert, great anxiety that the earth be fruitful, and in the story of Isis' search for her husband's body this anxiety is given coherence and meaning.

When Alexander conquered Egypt to found the city which was named after him, there came together Greek thought models and Egyptian practice, which gave birth to alchemy. Precious texts were lost at the Library of Alexandria in 46 BC when Julius Caesar set fire to the city. Thus we will never know the inner truth that informs the myths and the great pyramids of Egypt. Christianity incorporated mythic elements of the early religions while the rational Greek mode of thought developed alchemy into science. With the Enlightenment, and the elevation of reason, came the final blow to the inner order in which religion and the earlier esoteric forms had sought a correspondence. With the acceptance of verification through entirely objective means, an inner lack of wholeness became the hallmark of our civilisation.
A modern Isis finds herself on the same search as her precursor in Egypt almost five thousand years ago.

Il n'est nulles laides amours ni belle prison

- Lord Herbert of Cherbury

CANTO 1

Mai non t'appresento natura o arte
Piacer, quanta le belle membra in ch'io
Rinchiusa fui, e sono in terra sparte.

Dante *Purgatorio* Canto XXXI

I climbed up a hill in Tuscany
Where illuminati set my seal in time
To wonder at the spirit I set free.

I didn't know mendacity, nor crime –
I was the innocent at Heaven's gate,
Beholding beauty, sacred and sublime.

My boyfriend with the powers couldn't wait
Until he was exhausted intimate
And took from me the goblet of my fate,

And as he couldn't even penetrate
The mystery of my body, he grew jealous
And spent his lust on me to perpetrate

Not the purity of wholeness in a zealous
Love in tune with Nature and with conscience,
But his own discourse with the entellus

Which split philosophy and science,
Discourse which was pallid substitute
For my mystical experience.

My commune with nature was made destitute:
This fragment of the wildness of my speech
Is history's reckoning to its broken root.

The maid is waiting by the manor's reach:
Betrayed twice over, she ran around the town
Naked in the truth she had to teach,

And liberty is palsied in her gown,
Her streeling hair betoken of the sinner -
Her love has gone, the gutter shows a crown

Rolling in mire, a headless twin to win her –
The centuries, a broken necklace in her hand
A marriage of life and death, Polyxena

In the bad-lands of myth, like canned
Music making dance bizarre, meet
No wings, find feeling has been banned.

Her true love is not able to greet
Her when he comes. Instead
A mossy paradigm under fleeing feet;

In the locker photo near her bed,
She keeps his secret, unsayable name
As the townspeople put curses on his head,

And she is left, as if alone, in shame,
They tell him lies, lies everywhere the same.

CANTO 2

The City is of Night, perchance of Death,
But certainly of Night.
James (B.V.) Thomson *The City of Dreadful Night*

The radios scream it must be raw to reach,
But my heart's a feather; it's not made of paste.
My lover was a lover, love's law to teach.

"Romance!" cries the vendor of the paper waste:
Romance is the bread that's sold by chunk,
A sailor's hoard of hard tack you can't taste.

A hero in chains like an honest punk
Bursts into manhood, not allowed to feel –
Life is doled out in slices, hunk by hunk.

I dreamed of him last night, it was a steal
Straight out of the morgue's ravening maw
I found my truth a living dream to heal;

My own dream gone to sail the ocean raw
Of eternity – he left me, his wife and sister:
I had not time to read to him the saw

Of promise, to wake him with the glister
Of my tear, to re-member, to call him to life -
For a proper leave-taking. The Twister

Stole the most expensive myth – I, his wife,
And he remembered me not. With outstretched arms
I comb this world of the dead, so rife

With the unravelling of my charms,
Who told black lics, I had been untrue?
My love, you went to death with false alarms

But I will find you, so I can be beside you
You sail in your eternal boat without my truth
I loved you, and I did not betray you –

I was faithful, lover of my youth!
Among these hopeless faces I might find
One that is not a mask, that has some ruth:

Is guide to your spirit. I'm blind
With the constant search in rubble and cement
Broken alleys, broken bottles, the unkind

Spirits throw down their litter to dement
The possible, they want to deny the rood,
Railing and grating will not relent

This quotidian squalor in a dream of wood:
A green tide, a seasonal faithful lurch,
For your body is a temple of the good.

Now I remember, your body was a church!
A broken chancel lodges in my heart
In the broken glass underfoot, I search

The way of nature, the whole inside a part,
And each part has its spin in history,
The earth itself the sun god's loving dart

His eye the universe and full of mystery.
Even these walking wounded hopeless dreamers
Could wake one day to find their true consistory!

But in love's absence they're all screamers
In a dry silent land, and wasted
Living corpses who are their own redeemers;

Worse than that, their rationale is pasted
Not with ointment, but with blood, the spirit
Of the living dead upon their heart has feasted,

Each breast canopic gourd, each union levirate,
Devouring endless widowhood in boredom –
Spirit's dead! What living world inspirit?

Spirit's dead, and all living is a whoredom!
My husband gone without a proper funeral,
A dead city remnant of his heirdom,

A citadel where love is corporeal,
The holy centre's gone, the world a shroud
A culture fossilised, supposedly liberal,

A winding sheet to re-collect this crowd!
Yet, I loved you so, infinity like a glyphic
Eternity lay behind us – I vowed

To trace our passion in legend and in diptych
Upon these walls the wording of our splendour
And time will not undo my hieroglyphic

Art set down so the gods can wonder –
That I win your soul back for this last farewell
To put the proper seal on what was rent asunder,

And write the truth, as I know, in speedwell
Ink and lotus flowering, belling
Not only our story, Osiris, but to seed well

The truth, our love did not begin by telling:
For before I met you, as virgin deflowered
In a lunar landscape, so my sad welling

Into womanhood, now with love empowered
I feel this pilgrimage just like my thirst,
For my heart with meteoric stones is showered!

When you held me in your arms, you were the first!
For this you're dead and it was my father's curse!

CANTO 3

Well, honour is the subject of my story.
I cannot tell what you and other men
Think of this life; but, for my single self,
I had as lief not be as live to be
In awe of such a thing as I myself.

Shakespeare *Julius Caesar* Act I, Scene 2

There is a pearl of water, that is wife
That whitens laws and shops cold syllogism
And grammar of love is wound with strife:

Like knotted plaited hair it is a blossom
Of ordered wealth for viewing and for use –
It falls down on the pillow like a besom,

And sister-wife carries in her loose
Garment an amulet to revive the dream.
A girl neophyte to the classics can peruse

In vain the lineaments of her scheme,
Failing to find her true love's form – galling –
(Not in the library or the football team!)

Her boy. His dark raven curls falling
Into the lake where he disappeared
To tap memory while his sister is calling

Out to him in dreams. It was weird
The way she caught him in the alcove's lamp
And of the wall made a tiered

Wedding cake for her record's amp
In which the symbol swords announced
The demise of love, the outlaw, and the camp.

Really, Isis. His head, severed, bounced
As a ball between players, which she, sole
Goddess, overcame and trounced.

But the schoolgirl vision sees him whole
And does not even notice his will to dismember –
Through her life, gradually, a flaky soul

Whose chips are her own, will ask her to remember
As each dishevelled dream hits the rocks,
That she had loved this god, a dry ember,

Now, of her most rapt being. She washes socks
And scours the pub, shakes the pillow
But he doesn't fall out. Instead, he blocks

Up the chimney where a burning willow
Sends smoky signals he is in particle
And on the road to Amarillo,

Where a bishop's protests were branded with the sickle
In this small American town manufacturing bomb
To turn the world to ash and icicle -

Form in the heart of the dove, a coulomb
Stranger and sadder than brokenness, the sap
Of a torn tree, a bleeding willow's maelstrom

In a desert of shame and guilt. Her lap
Holds the one between – their child –
Her apron forms the useful pap

Yet this girl refused the role. Wild
As the last lament of Isis, poured
Honey on her throat and men beguiled,

While she loved only one. He, hoard,
Where image was the god, the all, the Lord.

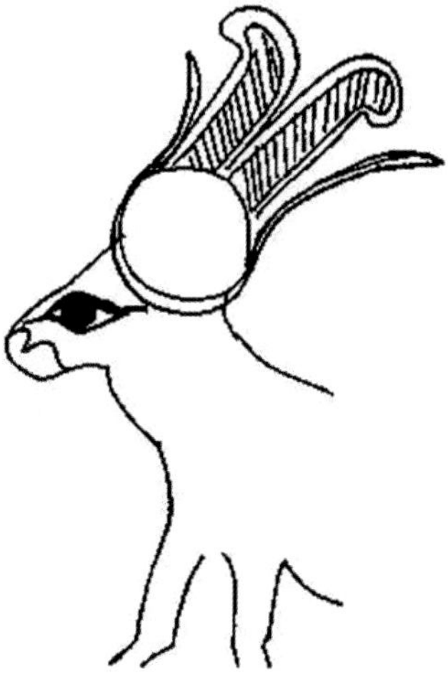

CANTO 4

Come ye forth,
Fallen fiends of heavenly birth,
That have forgot your Ancient love,
And driven away my trembling Dove
For you shall bow before her feet;
You shall lick the dust for meat;
And though you cannot Love, but Hate,
Shall be beggars at Love's Gate.

William Blake *The Everlasting Gospel*

Dawn. City of the dead. Graffiti
Scrawled on grey cement tell the legend,
A girl in headscarf, passing – Nefertiti

Without her consort. For a white second
Pregnant, she is held among the giving
Beautiful, and the Necropolis fecund

As a wreath at the funeral of the living –
But they're shut in, hopeless, wry-eyed –
In your artist's scrawl, write misgiving;

The only release, death. Dry-eyed,
Born into a broken myth, an onion
Without its rich interior, lye-eyed

As the happy somnambulist is disproven
In the marks on his skin, now worn
Lush as the tale of some duped escutcheon:

And the delivery vans blow the horn:
Frozen nursery rhymes render to the deaf –
"Green Sleeves" – the classics dipped in scorn.

How can he be punished, who left her bereft
Left her stretched, as if a preying bird
Had fed on her heart, and her spirit cleft?

Her true love writing in hieroglyphic word;
Teeming creation mastered the stylus grip
And left neat decoration on the surd.

His cosmic humour, and his astral trip,
One-eyed king in the country of the blind,
Is he hiding in a comic strip

Or pop song, this stripling? But to find
Putrefaction, where living dead
Die from pride of a bacon rind

When supper refused? Who has bled
Inwardly through the ages, word-bound
Orisons in millennia who led

Sister search for his corn body, round
As the men who walk now, chipped
Into portions like each raw piece found

While he dismembered and his sister shipped
On the banks of the Nile, searching
For trace and fragment, and her heart tripped

Each time a red corner showed, and she lurching
In reddish sands for the real story –
Her soul failed at melody, at churching.

Still, in the wincing fragments of the whole glory
Of the song that trembled on the still river
And when she heard chords darken, saw the gory

Field and seeping hut, their sundering, and the quiver
Of herself alone in the almost ochre
Soil, the song became cacophony and a shiver

Took hold of her, and lamentation. Some joker,
He who jerked his wet dream of existence
Into fullness, tore her apart and woke her

To the separation of the night and the persistence
Of division and the eternal other
Where one must choose love, or else subsistence,

And on that choosing, die for love of brother!
So wept, and she a fragment found
At each tear, and as a new-made mother

Is enraptured in creation's love and sound
She sang a song to Osiris, her true informed
And only love, her half, her round

And in her vestigial tear an image formed
Which remains now in the dream of every girl
Who first sees her true love.   Confirmed

By pop song and the dancing whirl
Of a young imagination in a famine,
He has the immortality of a pearl,

Just like pearls that drag from the stamen
To mirror microscopically the web of life,
He is pearl, shell-pearl, and her man.

"I wept tears, the shape of my eye. I, his wife
And he remembered me not, yet his nod
Was my eye, and truth and I were life!"

Vestigial intaglio of the golden rod,
True love, first, only and last,
He would be a fraction of a god –

For her God was broken on a cross and past
His constancy she could see no diurnal
That was not filled with pain, so cast

Each mode into the day of eternal
And imperishable beauty, rich as Croesus
In tingeing with the miraculous the kernel

Of truth, which lay broken into scintillating pieces;
So the lovers' beauty drew the pieces in
Each golden fragment was a coin for Jesus,

Or Jesus' poor: to keep earth clean, to pin
A glance on healing, and beauty
Sealed up the magic jar of sin.

Such pennies shall be given as a duty
To kick the Devil, and to pester him forever
Until he disappears from the cutey-

Pie notions of evil, his dust must never
Touch us, he took down the tree
The fruit, and love and God did sever.

In the act of creating there was me
Born, and you. And we are since apart.
Sisyphus is toiling to find the key

Under the stone he is rolling from his heart,
Inscribed by Lucifer who once loved light
And stole from Egypt their good destiny:

Geography and astronomy, a test of sight
Never inscribed on stone, and still he lurks
To render into ashes the alchemy of light

The arches of ages, and God's works.
Until such time as he can be rolled
Up, and made to do without his perks

Let him be sealed up, and as is told
He will be cast into fire, forever burnt
Giving God energy for what is foretold.

So, the light-bearer loved night and sunburnt
The hopes of young girls, and the icon
Of love had to be painfully unlearnt.

Love in action is when he has his bike on,
The will to romance can make good turn ill;
Confusing love and the image is a Reichian

Dissonance, an addict's desire, in the mill-
Race of being a sojourner is pert
Postponing of the inclination of the will

To latch on to sensuous pleasure in the hurt
Of being ground to nothing in an also-ran
Drama of sex, not love: curt

Like a doorbell summons and the tables then
Laid, and forgotten, a hasty meal
Leaving objects strewn outside the pen

Of domestic cage desiring what must be real.
We never can desire what others can desire,
We can never fully accept what they feel,

And so it ends when love dies in the fire
And dreams a butchery of what is becoming,
Because others fasten on the widow's pyre

Of burnt-up useless love, in that summing
Up there greens a dream of honour,
Away from the useless history, the coming

Of those who hate women as lover,
Who can only imprint their lust on broken
Daydreams, and stamp the seal of summer

In a hidden cache where sentiment is token
To take away a father's curse, a lyric
Fresh as her stress, unspoken:

As before her first kiss a rainbow empiric
-al lit the page, put flesh on love's emotion
Open and tender, as if the Pyrrhic

Dance of the first explosion and commotion –
The billionth, billionth, billionth second before matter
Formed in the universe, and frozen action

Whose epitaph was beauty, and honour the latter
Day saint of greatness before entropy set in –
Spirit was. Before fusion and the batter

Of time and space stretched galaxies to thin
Spirals of coruscating light, cartwheels
Fizzling on existence like discarded skin

Of God's first protracted impulse and reels
Of love in His fishing rod and net
As souls are gathered into rainbow creels

So this moment before love began. Yet
There was honour, resplendent, pure and bright
Before even the mind began to get

Drunk with pain. Forget, beget, plain get, the blight
Of her father's curse a harpoon to inertia, the task
Of naming separation, discrimination, in dark night,

Still honour stood fast, in time, in galaxies to bask
With all the soul's intention upon God
To tear from the soul's demeanour the mask

Of material being, to be a shining rod
Where goodness is measure, sole
Impulse, measure itself, and pod

To hold the deeds in, like the whole
Green case where peas bed down together
Separate, heads in a bed, yet whole;

As the certainty when the feather
Was weighed against the heart, a universe –
In Egypt a confident mood, no wether

Of imagining, but love, then, to disburse
Throughout the ages infinite largesse –
Between will and creation, came a curse

To fall upon the plans. Yet his caress
Was sent to mend separation, and the night
That followed day, a love to bless

Unite division between seen and sight,
Man and woman, ugliness and beauty
To bring to creation a unity in right;

But such love depends on chance, is no duty
And when we see our partners, we may choose
To love or leave them, mask our sooty

No. We may embrace, or choose the blues –
Be dissident, seek husband, wife, whether
To pour into one person our aspiration's cues.

In the hanging shadow of this tether,
The preference for the real glitters,
Constantly homeless, a desert tribe, rather

Like a sacred story whose bitters
Are annealed as a rhyme into logos:
And the cataleptic calypso critters

Who burn the texts and cry a bogus
Holiness, who shirk the real encounter,
Are more interested in gesture than in focus.

The curse of her father an old counter
Flip side madonna, B side whore,
Dropped into darkness, who would count her:

A physical being where matter was the core?
Sweet form by the candle, true self by the door.

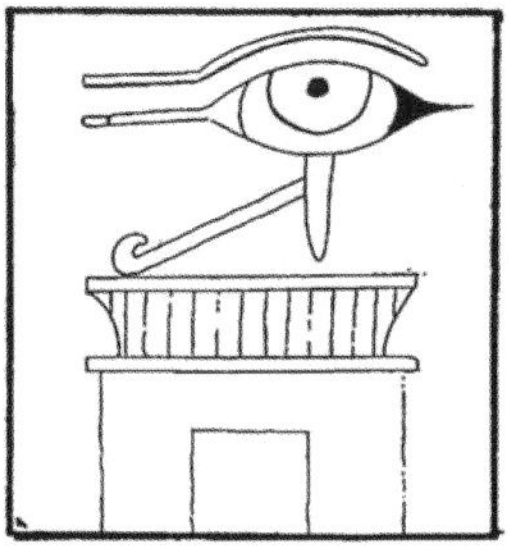

CANTO 5

Poi cerchiaro una pianta dispogliata
di giori e d'altre fronda in ciascum ramo.

Dante *Purgatorio* Canto XXXII

An eye of the all-god appeared on the tree,
An eye of the all-god appeared on the date-palm,
A powerful god was going to be.

A powerful one, who might subdue like calm
A powerful one, he raged until he was burnt
Yet supreme, his eye kind as a balm.

He created Time that darkness might be learnt
Slowly, he curbed the dark demons
While angels cheered the heart with referent.

Light grew like an orange, paled like a lemon,
Good as a midge's belief in my mouth
His tongue blessed the real, the tough, the leaven.

"I am the spirit eternal, North and South
East and West, I make air to breathe and sing
My soul is creator of the world, a youth

Loved by the other is my mystery and my ring.
I create order by thinking that I live –
Evil is underfoot, I do not see a thing:

Only the whole, and my order can give
Law to the world, to shape reality
Out of my mouth come images that sieve

The shape of genius it is good to see,
The shape of goodness that there is no separation,
The shape that makes perfect love of you and me.

There is no evil in the heart:
No matter how small the flock
I, the Lord, will care for each part;

But in troubled times such faith will rock,
Be destroyed by those who do not understand:
Bad men lived, and I cursed not their stock!

I would have destroyed the heirs by my hand,
But my own seed! How I wept to see
The evil of my own making the world bland.

I wept, for such sickening perfidy
A whole generation came to harm, bidden
The real nature of things to break harmony.

Soon the clear river was a foul midden
The men of violence had a wish to kill,
So goodness became secret, became hidden,

The constant shifts concealing in the mill
Precious stones, waiting for bright water
When the banks will crumble, stopping ill."

And the tongues of heaven crying, "O daughter
Down the ages we have seen you, dark.
The real story we would hear, so laughter

Can break free again, from the bark
Of the hounds of hell, free from the abominable
Pain of centuries' silence, sail your barque

Into a golden age now past imaginable.
We who have chopped our lives into token,
Is it possible that this daily, interminable

Calling away of our images, to broken
Dreams, is the brick housing of our spirit
The real pain is that we live in the unspoken,

Forever finding fragments only which inspirit
Us, who search in the ruin of our past,
Yet each finding asks the question, we inherit

What? We are heirs to plaster cast,
Plastic moulding, moving statue, neon crib,
At each electric dawn we are enthusiast,

By sunset realize we're built upon a fib:
A gloss on happiness, a pagan coin-op
Through which we stumble blindly, to ad-lib.

But imagine that every day is like an air-drop,
Creation in a grain of sand a rhyme –
The whole day a god! Religion non-stop!

Each movement of the eyelid a mime!
And every action a sacred ritual.
No one would ever dare to talk of time

Passing, but each word weighed and spiritual,
And in each name hidden the secret soul,
A holy name for all that is habitual –

Like the babe imagines the world entirely whole!
Each casual sound charged with meaning,
Mother a goddess, father no token role!

Each breath significant, no mask demeaning,
Putting the whole spirit into creation,
Making each thought a very greening,

The secular world a poor outmoded station:
Each person a mystery without name,
But named, what spiritual elation!

Reeling through space like a weird computer game,
Or rampant satellite with nodes a quiver,
The centre's missing, the feelings just the same.

So kids press buttons. But they never shiver
Their mouths turn down with boredom's shibboleth
Their elders have sold them down the river

Like Osiris long ago was sold by Seth
Two brothers who became each other's rival:
The soap opera of the Egyptian jet set.

Their sky mother, Nut, on arrival
At puberty, no child for her predicted
Naturally concerned about survival,

She felt her father, the god, had derelicted
Duty, so that she should not bring forth.
He dreaded being supplanted, was afflicted:

So rained his curse on her – henceforth
She would be barren to the end-odd.
The resourceful woman went to Thoth,

The god of wisdom, and the moon god,
Challenged him to chess, and won this:
Five days of moonlight, five children in the silver hod.

Osiris, Harmachis, Isis, Seth and Nephtys
Five extra days to the solar year,
Five days of silver for a golden kiss,

Five extra days, and the showy spear,
The absolute crown, the universe, was shattered.
The mother's eye began to shape like a tear.

She kept her silence, none of this mattered,
The secret mime behind the veil still held,
And not an ounce of holiness was scattered:

But five splendid beings the god beheld.
He got older, he dribbled at the mouth –
Isis and Osiris longed to weld

And have a child, but could not do without
The help of Ra, so Isis gathered up the spittle
Fashioned a cobra to warn of drought,

So when Ra saw the cobra not a whittle
He cared, so hurt with the wound of the snake,
"Tell me your secret name, for marital

Purpose, I need to transfer the take.
I'll breathe it to no-one,
There's differ between the real and the fake."

Down the ages fake children fool no-one
But real girls often go amiss
Looking for their true love, someone

Who will be lover and brother, who will kiss
Away modernity and the illusion of the human,
Who will take them through the window, to miss

The cosy domestic life imprinted on the besom,
The quiet coupling that is a quiet pain –
The life that's dead to everything save the blossom

That promises the spirit eternal life again;
But search too hard beneath the balcony,
The wolf may find her first, in the dark rain,

And in her chordless virgin euphony
Try to kill her before she meets her hope,
Before she can cast away the litany

Of fresh dreams, knitted like a rope,
To help her over the balcony, into the realm
Where down below, he's dead from too much dope.

From the beginning, life is such a game.
Bound to lose. Her mother was the same.

CANTO 6

Love bade me welcome; yet my soul drew back,
Guilty of dust and sin.

George Herbert *Love*

Those evenings by the dim lamp of the street,
She shored up what fragments might have bound her,
And dreamt a future husbanded and neat.

The gangly arms of boys were not around her
As she studied Euclid (Pass) and convent lace,
The gloss on happiness could still confound her,

For in the family's transcript from their race,
A hidden beauty lay inside the dream
Of aspiration. There was distance in her face:

A possibility that could hurt the scheme.
A frozen virgin by the window pane,
A dent in 'perhaps' to blur the 'seem'.

Her childhood gifts of quickness, and a brain
Provided she did not use it, quite a farce,
Making her life troubled in the main.

No matter if she were the smartest in the class,
The nuns made her wait last to take her prize
– An honours student made for a pass –

In case she might be vain, the size
And fount of every sin was pride,
As the Devil is the father of all lies.

Reared with music, her father's side
Were bards, and prophets with truths to tell
In a country were faith had never died.

But the nuns punished her under the Angelus bell,
Consigned outside the lavatory where each boy
Could stick his tongue out at her. Spell

Words she might, yet she was their toy;
To the fixed notions she must be sacrificed
So learning must be painful, not a joy.

She stood there, and eternity spliced
At the centre was her soul:
She was with God, and she had diced

Against the formless shadow of the whole
World, and in its transient state
She felt the terror of the flesh roll

Against each protruding tongue, and hate
Poised itself on the windowsill of her heart,
Begging to be admitted and be accounted fate,

To vindicate a child. Truth an art:
She would not let it be, but instead
Refused the poison of the liar's dart.

But there was one little boy who said
No. In her dreams he wore a kilt
And cuddled her when she was sad in bed:

She would dream each night that he would lilt
Her favourite tune – "Lord Gordon" – till she slept.
With songs like this her heart would never wilt

But kept her going through the dark ages, leapt
Like a giddy phantom over the abyss
That was her youth, when she often wept

For ideals reduced to rubble, and a kiss
Of lust could turn her heart to ash,
An insect king atop the anthill bliss.

And yet, her emblematic hero – no rash
And token admiration – but daring to say no –
Gave her the hope that truth was no lash,

But beauty, too. And she would grimly sew
Her squares of cotton, token stitches
Like elephants' teeth – booty long ago

Made domestic. And the wild ditches
Rife with blossom. She herself kept
The dark broom cupboard of her hitches

With the past. Then how she wept,
For her treasures on the clothes line
One night in a fairy gale were swept

Away. And the Inspector's two slaps, fine
On pitched domesticity gone awry,
While other girls showed neat squares – nine

Stitches in a row, ironed like a cry
Of suppressed rage, where the latches
Of information left many a why,

And neat thread bitten off. Her patches
Left unanswered questions at the hem:
The farmyard where the hen scratches

For food was closed forever from them.
Ladies not to shrink from washing up
Would be frozen in the requiem

That was history's verdict on their coming up
To flower in mid-century. They'd be wives
Trained to use their talents for the sup

History could pour on their heads. Quiet lives
For their ruler, undoubtedly male. In a few
Of these girl-children, though, the dream revives.

In church, Mother pinned her to the pew
With rough nails. Four red crescents
And the cross remaindered by the churchyard yew.

Throughout all this, remaining quiescent
Praying for the souls on the brass plaque,
Enjoying purgatory and the incandescent

And kindly rage of God. Mother's back
Bent in her new coat. It was 'forty-seven
The famine's centenary. And the lack

Of love as a giant man in heaven
Empty and sick of what he gorged upon,
Envious in the threshold of being riven

Between earth and hell, still a pawn
Between spirit and matter – the eternal tussle
Of daisy, and grass, and sunlight on the lawn –

A summer's day where filaments can rustle
Like an angel's wings beating out a hymn
And their flight in the magic and puzzle

Of being. So Mother's fists, the rim
Of a physical whole abandoned
Sweet, short, sharp tears would not limn

A prayer-book with light. A marshland
Of exotic blooms grew inviolate
And their lush beauties would be hard to husband.

Her young swelling breasts reprobate
Her mother called the nurse, it must be cancer
Such growth of beauty in a girl, extenuate.

The nurse smiled gently with the proper answer:
"Normal development", and her smile benign
Lit up the darkness. A Spanish dancer

Making colourful dresses swirl upon the line
In motion, yet stillness had possibility
And the nurse's smile, duende. A sign

Even when cowering, shy, a proband
On the verge of adolescence, limbs quite sleek,
She might be a dancer. In the bath, a saraband.

But Mother forced the door open so she could peek
At the showing forth of what to her was least,
The putting on of womanhood, as if in meek

Acquiescence to Nature's purpose and her feast:
Mother still felt the whole thing was vicious,
Tearing women between the angel and the beast.

So fled from her who with meretricious
Sleight of mind drew picture so repugnant,
There was no meeting point between delicious

Anticipation of true love and this unguent
Which nightmare furnishes as she. Un-nourishing,
Yet she, become she, and what was tender, poignant,

In spirit, mind and body hoped for flourishing
But soul was condemned to hunger amid sweetmeat:
In real life dreams, dreams ravishing and dervishing.

And so she sought the dark, ever sweet
Through a glass, a young man not so coy
Whose black hair made her grind her feet

Inside her shoes, oh he was such a joy,
A waif, born in freedom's evanescence
And she would dream she'd love this boy,

Until time threw a figurative essence,
A Greek vase with real flowers entwined
In their hair and in their heart's incandescence.

But the factory hooter and the school combined
To eke the dream out in darkness, stir
With a thick spoon of mistrust the lined

Calls of the popular song. And a blur
Like a flame warmed by two hands
Left civilisation like a tamed cur

Inside the walls of culture, and bit the bonds
Of love and friendship till they were a snare.
Songs were forgotten. In the native lands

Maybe a snatch of melody, like a hair
Unloosed from a headband, would lightly fall
Into the spaces where once lived a prayer.

How can a dream of despair be all?
Lighting is cigarette in the dark,
He leaned, a Teddy Boy, against her hall.

In the flood of the future, he was Ark
– definite refusal to acknowledge
That learning was anything but the bark

Of mad dogs in the abyss, and that college
Conferred respectability on the fake
Conferred authority upon the spoilage:

She would have gone with him, gone under
The hill like the dancers in the song
But he refused to take her. Torn asunder,

Her faith in him misplaced and she was wrong
Both to love learning and despise its use,
Especially to think, that for her the gong

And knell of history would let loose
A chime of freedom in this underworld,
Where repetition of chilled fate was the ruse

By which the gods defeated innocence, and hurled,
Into the blood and thunder of the race,
A flag to show that destiny unfurled

On grim silence. And face to face
The words dropped, crumbs at a feast
Inedible, and poisoned with a trace

Of hope. All would turn bitter
Her least twinge of liberty, palsied, still
In the ravening maw of the great beast

Who swallowed the universe like a pill,
Before the babe could stutter now: "I hope,"
Choking before he brought to birth: "I will."

So this dark young man, a smoky dope
Quenched by definition in his class –
Boxed, strait-jacketed – couldn't cope

With the social strata. He couldn't pass
Examinations as she did, but could only feel,
Like a wish disappearing in a well, a lass

As lithe as he in body, and he could peel
The layer of education off her like a shroud
And dance. (At her father's wedding feast the reel

Had sealed up magic in the stamping heel.) Proud
He couldn't bend to undo her enchanter,
Instead, he held her gently while the loud

Music told him he was king. The banter
Of centuries' untruth sealed his lips. Measured
By the accretions of the ages, the last canter

Of the centaur on the hills, a treasured
Perfection like a fly in amber
A single dance expression, and leisured

Silence the key. And the ruck and camber
Of straitened maidenhood the faulty tower
He would not scale, and would only clamber

Among the rubble and the fern of her power,
The intimation that the past was reborn
When she was handed to the ancient dower

Of grace in servitude, what he could only scorn.
Since he too was bound in space and time,

The living out of love would be forlorn,
So he rejected her. Her crime –
Intelligence. And her love of rhyme.

CANTO 7

le beau ne peut être la voie ni de l'utile
ni du bien, ni du saint; il ne conduit qu'à
lui-même.

Victor Cousin: lecture at the Sorbonne
on truth, beauty and the good.

So, spurned and virginal, she bounded off to greet
A theoretician who saw dialectics as the key:
That she should meet him showed that fate was neat.

He offered explanation, and she was free
Of love, perdition and the gargoyle hope:
Instead of hope, endless cups of tea.

This Marxist expiator of the dope
Of history was a shrewd conniver,
Trying for conversion, he would grope

At private parts. A professional skiver,
He scorned honest effort and a job,
A technicality like the Royal Liver

Of Art and Culture which were hocked to fob
Off the inquisitors at the Gates of Doom,
Poetry was the matter of the mob

And in his Credo there wasn't any room
For individual vision, nor personal feeling –
They were woven in the capitalist loom

And if she mentioned love, he hit the ceiling.
Or rather, collapsed from the Bohemian bed
Where discourse of this kind was peeling

Like paint in a hothouse garden shed,
Where plants wilted and were soon forgotten,
And carried like shrapnel buried in the head

From which regular nightmares were begotten.
And day turned into night, and year to year,
And still they argued till the core was rotten:

The last egg thrown at an orchestra, fear
Remaining to fill a vast emporium:
A wasted youth that finally cost dear.

They had their last real argument in the Forum
Of Earl's Court. Emigrants, they walked about
And were roped in to make a quorum

On the question – what is love's doubt
But that authenticity doesn't exist?
A rapier thrust that ran in and out.

Some were amused, and some were quietly pissed,
And she shouted and she ran away to the dark
Alley where real lovers kissed.

She came upon jazz music – as a lark
Might greet a nightingale in hell,
She entered in: here she might find her mark.

Here all lovers gathered, before the bell
Could summon them from paradise and show
The world the bliss which they could scarcely tell.

Café des Artistes! It was touch and go,
Here was a place she might be herself –
Vestige of her first love would row

Her across the Styx where Marxists on the shelf
Of history glittered with evil brain:
Just for an evening she would renew the Guelph

Inheritance in exile, and this stranger to the main
Formation of her being, asked her to dance awhile.
He was agreeable, tanned, and very sane.

He danced with her, and beamed his toothy smile
He asked her if she'd like to have a Coke,
And spoke about the flooding of the Nile.

Concerned, a gentleman, and afraid to poke
An elbow in the wrong place, he showed respect
Expressing laughter when she told a joke.

He gently said that she should reflect
Carefully before travelling home solo:
He had a car, which she might like to inspect –

White and shiny, the maker's metal logo
Polished and pert on the bonnet. She said "Fine",
But if he had ideas, it was no go.

He understood, nodded: an imaginary line
Lay between them as they rode the night.
She remarked on the pale quiet moonshine

That was nothing in his face. It was all right.
He was a gentleman, all she could ask,
Given as she was to ravages and blight.

Then, as she looked, she perceived a mask
In the murky reflection of the glass:
A speedy exit then became her task.

He sensed fear, and put his foot down on the gas.
The countryside loomed like a mad raven;
Clawing the rope of truth to find it pass

Into the realm of the impossible. He stopped, craven,
Outside a deserted house. There was no one
Not even a ghost of what was home and haven.

It was the place of rape. There was no gun
But the final clicking of the lock
Which said, "the sooner over, sooner done;

And what will happen will forever mock
Your dreams of loving and joy,
And dances on vases will no longer shock

You with the idea of bliss. A toy,
Trifle, thing – your inside, and your trust
Violated for ever. Don't be coy –

You asked for it. You are a woman, must
Know how things are. If you hurt,
If you say you're wounded by my lust,

I don't even want you. I'll be curt
This half an hour of painful sex
Will prove woman is just a piece of dirt,

And I am here to show you that you vex
Me, and all men, with your pretension.
What good is learning, when you can hex

Us with your power – now in declension.
Destroyed at the centre of your being,
You might enjoy it but for the tension

Of your being degraded. Now you're seeing
It all happen like a strange inversion.
Your love of beauty a fleeing force

But subject to my perversion."
Finally he crumpled to a tissue
As if he had proven his assertion.

He drove her to the Marxist,
Who allowed it might be a catharsis.

CANTO 8

The brazen throat of war had ceased to roar,
All now was turned to jollity and game
To luxury and riot, feast and dance.

Milton *Paradise Lost,* X1, 713

To be in pain is to feel a different
Metaphor for the seeking of one's dream
In anxious lands, like England, there's no referent;

So cracks the heart, and Irish blessings seem
To be exiled in the skiff of doom
Running downstream like a faulty beam

Cracked from a cathedral, and in the gloom
Of the Middle Ages and the sanctuary bell
Tolls a truth where women have no room

So, brought up in father's shadow, who can tell
If paradise is meant for girls and daughters,
When so many feel they're a present he must sell

To the highest bidder, so the dark waters
Close around her head like a barque forbidden,
Drowned in the miscreant time when she falters

And subterranean, she comes bidden
To erotic fantasy like a plague of guests,
To eat the heart's wisdom in the midden.

A rape is her fault. Those pests
Of men knew she was putting out –
Those blood wounds on her head – crests

Of the cockerel, who knew beyond doubt
She was his to master and possess,
Be he Prince Charming or common lout.

Now she belongs to no-one, and a caress
From her is the prerogative of many
And what she has left to give no one can bless:

The next time she meets a man she'll be more canny,
She won't look for a broken god between his eyes
Even if he starts to act quite zany-

Her gaze will dart away, and a disguise
Of hardened liberation will be her attraction.
She chooses no disguise, she can't tell lies,

And in her life account book makes subtraction,
Leaves out like a black hole solemn gifts
Of self to self, honour, and abstraction.

And so in her heart there grows a rift
Of thirteen moons, a constant wheeling
Hers and not hers becomes a place where lifts

To the soul take place, for a kind of healing.
Romance, capitalist romance, is the chief bait
And from shop to shop, soon she's reeling

From lecture hall to launderette, consumed with hate:
The most ideal child in the school becomes
The plaything of the furies and the fates.

She gets a buzz from scalding desert bums
Who mix up love and commerce, profit and work,
Soon her life with material rhetoric hums

And she does not, she finds, shirk
From tea, or love in the afternoon,
Her self absent. As if her soul can lurk

Among cheap volumes of a reckless swoon,
Where librarians issue volumes on a kiss
Until the denouement of the honeymoon.

Lies, lies. Marxists speak of postponed bliss –
Jargon, a currency to shape the world
Until every truth was a dumb and broken hiss.

The story nestles with her makeshift herald,
As a bird, headless, seeks to gather ruin.
The rhetoric span while her cries whirled

In the air like tongueless feathers. To win
An absentee landlady with a pen
Is easy when false prophets pay to win

And hate starts at home. Here's a den
Where stratagems poke like a stick through bars
And new beginning a diviner for a fen

Of stagnant waters though life was holy:
She was a vessel for her life's mission's sake,
And she could feel the hurt of not being wholly

Human, just as the foetus swims in dark lake
Of amniotic fluid, and was blind
To the registry office, the wedding with no cake,

Flowers, nor prayers – a borrowed ring. Not a kind
Thought passed between the unfortunate pair,
As spinster became matron, and the book was signed.

A pub like a long hall in the West End, the snare
Closing in, a horrible noose. A peck
From the vulture, and a missing prayer.

And so, the craft of herself is now a wreck,
Spread-eagled on the future she has truck
With all the notions that a soul can speck

Before she yields herself to cosmic muck
She must refuse her honeymoon, try to wedge
Herself between the squandering and the luck

Of a divided goal. He had the edge
On this, his father was from Ulster
And had thrown the mother off a window ledge

Back in the USA. And he could bolster
Her in her eye's defiance, firmly fix
Death on her like a six-gun holster.

At the wedding feast, his cautious licks
At the cake would make it thin, and he fatter –
In the rented room, there was a crucifix

And a decade gambolled in colours, the matter
Of all the Marxist's scorn and use.
She left the feast because she felt the patter

Of raindrops on the skylight to fuse
Into a dance with the bandsman – a troubadour.
He brought her to the sea, so she would lose

For ever her notions of matter and the *uaireadoir.*
She saw the dance of Shiva in the sand
And returned to the hotel as to a corridor

Of pain. They passed by a hot-dog stand
And she ate a sausage and it hurt –
The rubbery meat was a physical band

That mocked her being. She threw it in the dirt
Watched a dog devour it and felt sick –
Eat or be eaten, the world's command was curt.

And when he asked her to take her pick –
A life with music, or a ceaseless natter –
Was there a choice? She left behind real quick

Her groom at the wake of spirit and matter.
In the hotel there were waiters buzzing.
Was this the happiest day, love on the batter?

And a new sound invented, here a dozen
Of sweet Beatles' lyrics were to be heard,
As if Bob Dylan hadn't been busy sussin'

The mood of the generation, and his beard
And curls a prophecy of rage,
As if the Bible could be writ without the Word,

So had she, as if he'd left a page
Watted like a cut-out, just from home,
The name for the nameless hurt each age

Tries to pin on its artists, and despite tome
On tome, the libraries of official truth,
The miles of books, the authority from Rome,

The real truth, a secret transmission, uncouth,
Which isn't spoken but is felt by youth.

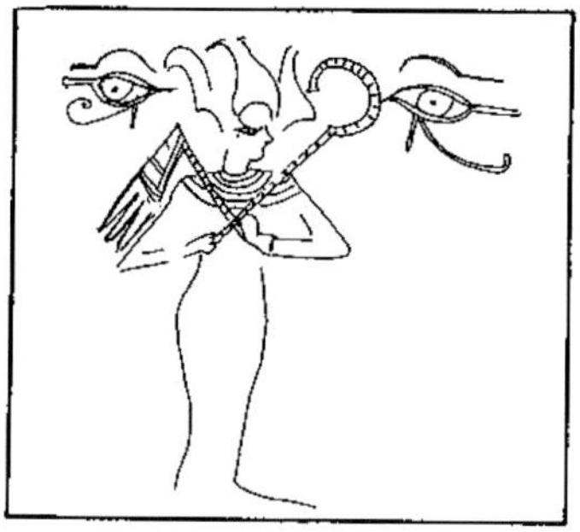

CANTO 9

The atrocious crime of being young I shall neither attempt to palliate or deny.

William Pitt, Earl of Chatham

Being young is understood by Indians who followed
Mother Nature as goddess and friend,
Letting good fall into the everyday hallowed

By intimate secret ritual, who can bend
Back the dark as he is in the streets' guts,
The virgin's paramour whose love will never end?

First love stays in her heart like the sleazy sluts
In big kitchens who nourish the world,
Past the familiar, into the ruts

And lane-ways of the intricate wood,
Where the pastures of clover are forsaken
For sweet drenching darkness and dry mud

And countless leaves reaching the taken
Fall, and falling into infinity as rotten
As the material barn where their shaken

History stops and cannot pass like cotton
Seed into the testicles and generate new life –
They must lie at the transverse, unbegotten

To the future, unremembered to the past strife;
Sweet and infinite with the need of their existence:
The ground below them is anguished and rife

With insects who burrow with persistence
Into the neat order of chaos and construe
A meaning for their life's fall, an assistance

To the stone philosopher who will spew
Out of his brain a web of words
Most being "I", and sometimes, "you".

He is as closed to the transmission of surds
As those leaves falling in a concrete well,
He finds logarithm in the chant of birds

But stiffens his ear to misspell
The aural transcript of Nature's way,
He's on a spiral, he's a dumb bell.

So her cardboard groom, love gone astray
Had left meaning out of the parlour game
Had levitated, because there was nothing else to say.

Hope was gone, and her auspicious name,
A navel cord torn out, would give her trouble,
She was the wild, who had become the tame,

Would she ever find her double?
What twin spirit would love her with delight
Be glad to consume this dream's rubble?

So she spun out existence like a night
Invading her soul in peerless squalor,
And she gave in because she had lost the fight

To begin with. Put to the pin of her collar,
Virginity's demise proof of her corruption,
One sin too many, and no matter that the dollar

Fluctuated on the stock exchange, wealth's eruption
On the carcass of society, that was no sin
In the ownership of people, the irruption

Into slavery, the buying and selling in
Of women to men in matrimony,
There was virtue, and virtue's prudent skin.

But outside the state of compulsory honey
There was no redemption, blessing or boon,
There is no value save the power of money:

Married, but having passed no honeymoon
Where was her real self, just to recover
Her lost soul, lost self, that still tune

In all the songs would be accounted for, discover
Male supremacy, stopping the power of women.
She found herself completely out of cover

Craving affirmation, love in a famine
As food to the starved. If she was OK
In bed, she was a true feminine specimen.

But who would win her in an ideal's bouquet,
A black hole in the universe of love?
To say the least, it was slightly *risqué*

What impeccable lover be allowed to shove
A delicious branch into her jet liner
Whom she would call her only turtle dove?

None. So it came about this sad regina,
Who had been dishonoured by a clerk
Betrayed to the consortium she was no diviner

Of accident than that horrid jerk
Who proved by force she was desirable
By the genus, man. Earned his trademark

And thereby showed that she was reducible
To a body, who could view the motions
Even making the wind and rain impenetrable;

And so for thirteen moons, the salty oceans
Heaved in answer to her silenced cries –
Pain more of pebbles, and the notions

The man had, that he could win the sighs
Of the trees, the sun's charioteering in the sky
The moon turned to stone with his lies,

And the music was a three-chord why.
She lost early friends, deep in sensation,
She blocked off dream with a loveless tie.

Mute save in the explosion of condensation
On the window pane which showed the heaving heart
You could say she envisaged compensation,

He was human, she was human, part
Of the whole of humanity which should be knit
Their limitation was a form of art,

And art that reduces art, a life to wit
Upon, the dance and dancer gone berserk
In a ritual that was denial of the bit-

Part of romance – personal love a jerk
Of the kneecap denying common good,
And setting choral angels out to work

In the factory of immediate returns for blood.
Payment was like crimson blobs in light
Revolving for not being what they should,

So angels wept blood tears, a sight
God the Son nailed on the cross envisaged
When he saw the chalice of the human blight.

So angels turned their back on two marriaged
Only by skin and moon, owning no fear
Are angels scabs, and love sacrilegious?

Have words reality? At last no tear
Disfigured her as she strove the thing to finish
Her heart had been deadened for over a year –

And why should I another sad tale embellish
With aught but words, when life itself is stopped,
As cry is torn when cry is but a blemish

And life itself the illness and ovum dropped
To meet a spermatozoon it should not:
Tempt the genes to mend a foolish slop

Of passion on lives' overkill, and spot
Heraldic saltire with the get of lust,
And block a human being because of a knot

Where there was no legal existence? Stardust
Cringed in the heavens at the murder of a lie
That was not matter. Death is a form of trust,

That asks no creditor nor spancelled why –
No matter that the wrenching of a man
Can be predicted by astrology in the sky,

So when the child is unborn, the planets scan
Horizons for a speck of life, disappearing, mute
As the stars falling in the silver pan

And shoals of asteroids, that comets shoot
Only to discover what they miss is love,
And children can't get born without a root

Of tenderness, caring, a creation-centred shove
Of gravity at the nipple of the world
A leaf in the mouth, and the flying dove.

When she left, his rage finally curled.
He sold the story to the "News of the World".

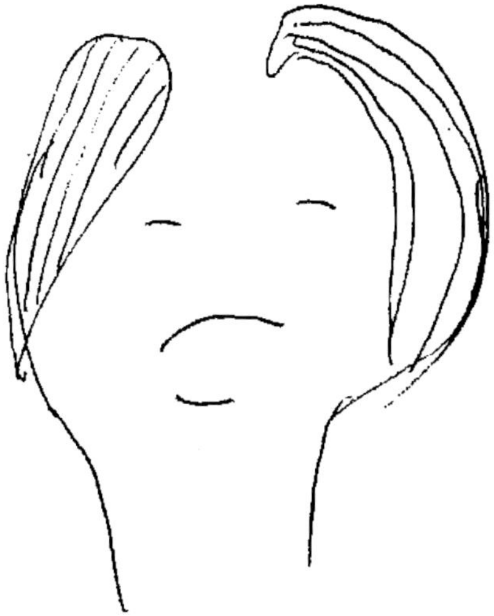

CANTO 10

The first casualty of war is truth.
Hiram Johnson: attrib. speech in US Senate 1918

How often longing, and her dream, a band
Around her head, tears begged, shed us, let us go
Scorched without rain like a desert land

A stubbled cheek he could plough and sow
In her heart plantation's wildest grief
Of human loss, her bitter task to know

Death. Death of one's child a loss, a leaf
Of a person never to be tree or wood
So she, that her head in a brief

Second signed a death warrant. Mood
Rose with the sun each day to damn the earth
Destruction rained upon her, like the hood

Of the eagle faces the abyss. A dearth
Of fear, a god-forsaking demurrage
On creation. And survival,

Birth of oneself. For with this marriage
Came shock. Still, refusing to the day
Its joys, its flowers, to finally discourage

All celebration. Her heroes gone away –
Dead, like Hendrix, Joplin, a hippy
Ethic. Scandal in the press. Who would pay

Informer's blood to redden the Mississippi?
Who would befoul blue river with rag of war?
Who would call peace lovers part of a recipe

For national disaster? And the slur and scar
Of this innovative generation never faded.
They stopped Vietnam. And the foreign far

Fields grew green again. But secret agents raided
Private intimacies for scandals about drugs –
Public interest was avid, then jaded.

After My Lai, who shrugs
Off a child's terror at a rifle?
The pain haunts still. And all the hugs

Children give, each sweet arresting trifle
Of human love, of course
End in a cry that will not stifle

Human cruelty. Every risk in love, and worse
Nightmare is part of loving one another
Pain and agony just par for the course.

The betrayals of lovers, all the bother
Of unrequited passion, pale to less
Than a mouth in that child's scream "Mother"!

And then, I am lacking. When I confess
That I am the child, the scream, the killer
Such tangled pain is not for me to bless

And upon the Byzantine pillar
Of forgetfulness, wreathe my head,
In the act's interval, life is just a filler:

A song in disarray can mean a thing
Beyond believing, a sweet inheritance
To puzzle out the secret of the ring

Of life and death, and love's munificence
In denying to all but the most detached
An understanding of its last admittance

Into the community of hope. Watched
By the vestal virgin of incompetence
Trusting in Nature's blueprints hatched

From the first explosion's transmittance
Of quintillions of atoms ready for the dance
The human offer to creation is a pittance

For the lease we call life, and every chance
Attends a history of a feeling
And every hope's a dust upon the lance

Of opportunity, or moving ceiling
Where death can wait, a figure in a balcony
Tossed on the human mob, and keeling

Over in the dance of life. Like alimony
Paid to the divorced – on a marble slab
He has the inscription and the testimony

And how he lusts at life. Like angels grab
Back the curtains of the world on Mondays
Wishing to be human, wishing to blab

And touch, after the ecstatic Sundays
To go AWOL and experience skin,
Go to the Zoo, and sip upon a sundae –

But they are angels, and they won't rush in
And they often sit on shoulders, and they weep
They turn their faces away at a sin.

On the horizon of the mortal there's a bleep
But we don't hear, we carry on with fervour
And a rustle at our elbow, a creep

Across the doorway. No human observer
Can match with scientific test the loss
Of an angel's presence on the favour

Of Holy Grace. A dialogue with the Boss
Reveals a show, mutely suffering
We are imaged in the figure on the Cross

And our materialist dream buffering
The essential prescience of the soul,
A votive candle, flickering, offering

In itself the pennies of the whole
As they thud in the brass box with a clatter
Fleeting golden moments in the role

Of truth, and jailed because in matter
There's no transference save in energy –
Who is going to set the coins to splatter

Red hot globules of matter in synergy
Proving existence consonant with essence?
A burst of flame, a raving liturgy?

A free expression in the right transcendence
Where object, subject, matter and mind and spirit
Are as one in a single splendid instance?

But history is slow progress. To inherit
The past is the burden of the dreamer
Who must disrobe at noon: the merit

Of the character a cyclorama
Where one dissects the passions of the race
In our bracing Western art, Karma

Considered unsuitable for mortals – to face
Head on, one's moral limitation
Is in the interest of a story's pace –

The moral fibre and heartbeat of the nation
Fixed in the culpability of an image
A goddess face in a woman of poor station

At the barricades. Her lost lineage
Shows the inversion of a once proud people
Who fought in hay-barns, with pitchforks – scrimmage

To defend the gold tongue and the iron steeple
The bell with iron clappers never mute
Since Patrick banished serpents, archetypal –

Energy, source, and female power, to boot.
But who has seen a figure on the cross
With breasts and belly, and a flower's root?

So write upon this page without a gloss
Only an angel understands the toss.

CANTO 11

Set me as a seal upon they heart
As a seal upon thine arm
For love is as strong as death
Jealousy as cruel as the grave.

The Song of Solomon

The broken chancel of her karma did not fade:
She left the pad with its instant passion,
Pinned a note to the mirror – 'Gone to get laid'.

It would finish the materialist off in his fashion:
She hopped onto a fresh landing, went to college
Found mind food in conversation, just a ration.

The second day spat out the germ of knowledge.
It flowered into a sheaf of poems, the owner
Had left it in a taxi with correct pollage,

His name, and number. Though he was a loner,
His verses read like smiles in deepest night,
A bird singing in the city said he'd 'phone her

And they met in "The Catacombs" by night.
Beneath the arches, their heads were put together
The old broken arches of the centuries' blight.

Now their heads were weighed against a feather,
They went to the cinema, where they viewed a rape
Two choristers who couldn't stand the weather

Of violent fact. They could no longer gape,
And outside told each other the whole story
The pain in their heads and hearts and nape,

How long they had been separate, the gory
Trail of hurt that dreams were put on sale,
Their cities that were devoid of glory,

So, like silver, their words fell into the pail
Of their rapt attention, sitting on the stair
Outside the cinema. A loud wail

Inside, the villain binding in his lair
Nailing faggots to the window with a hammer.
She remembered she could no longer dare

At life, but had become a college crammer:
And epistemology had made her body wince –
He said he'd throw rapists in the slammer.

They spoke in silences that held the hints
Of agony they knew – no easy guess,
And it cost them – new to love – what must evince

Signs of recognition so they would bless
The diligence of the Creation for the declension
To human pain when life is such a mess.

For him, the years of suicidal intention
In New York slums like a fallen king were fenced
Into a life of poverty with no subvention –

The treasure hunt in books of lives intense,
The unselectivc philosophy when the truth,
Too real, had stripped them bare in rents,

And they gave away their precious youth,
Perusing legend for a clue of honour,
Debased and cynical and without ruth

Everyone they talked to full of rancour –
Street corner merchants said they'd choose the dole
Rather than be big business anchor.

To be honest in a century when the soul
Had no existence save in illuminated script,
To love beauty, when everyone denied the whole,

The miraculous shimmer in the shape to shift,
The luminous centre at what could not be heard.
At the banks they rarely caught the drift

But dirtied beautiful rivers so the bird
Of history sank below the tide to kill
Any possible becoming of the word.

They walked as dreamers into the beautiful day
The hours passed and they were making hay.

CANTO 12

In the land of Egypt where we sat by the fleshpots
and when we did eat bread to the full.

Exodus 16:3

Now, nothing could separate the pair:
A blissful night together, when for ever
They were bound in one mystical prayer

As their skins touched, as if never
Again thread be boundary, or field
Be mapped and still not sever

The golden rain that fell. They wheeled
Together in a sacred dance, his first
Faith in woman restored, and healed.

Who would think that next, a thirst
From a patriarchal opposition would betray
This night of tender loving, and burst

The skin of romance as a pecking jay
Worries ripe fruit until he engorges
The autumn's blessings in a single day?

Even a minute of complete love enrages
Serpents and devils and raging queens
Who in each encounter, masquerade forges

A hole in their balcony of dreams,
Leaving prejudice on the windowsill, like crumbs
For stranger to finger as they hide their fears.

Such offering to the gods from sneaky bums
Of life, who despise talking, and feast
On the offering snatched away by thumbs

Of the agile boy whose laughter is creased
In the ridicule of angel's heart-stopped
Blithe encounters when devil's tricks have ceased –

But to spoil a young love! Here is cropped
Just after sowing time, to burn
Its credentials, its flower head lopped

By diligent cunning, planted lies, to turn
A young man's heart to cinder.
First, get him away from the cairn

Of pebbles he has strewn around her tender
Breasts, where their sweet scents
Were mingled. And the breath of slander

To disturb the lovers, like the unpaid rents
Of the basement apartment pounding on the walls,
Make them rise with guilt. Their clothes like tents

Confining the rash hang-ups to the calls
Of love and endearment, swopping places,
They surface in the sacred hall of halls,

Amid graffiti, tins, and traces
Of drunks, pungent, inarticulate
As the unspoken promises, and graces

In the air between them commensurate
With the time they have been given –
Aeons and eternity to obliterate

Every last vestige of one another. Riven
No more, their breath in their fire.
They are one, they cannot in their oblivion

Ever go back to being separate, but higher
Than earth's visible choirs they sing
Quietly of love, and self on the funeral pyre.

The motor bike outside, a chariot whose wing
Needs kicking to start the motion; she, astride,
Asks him to wait until she starts the thing.

She sits, pert, on the saddle, her skirts wide,
Hitched up and out of the wheel's way. She broods
Quietly on his past. Have angels lied?

Don't look back, but quietness is a mood
That begs the past, stay! If I am alone
Time is not consonant with good.

She brings her bike to life, why should she moan
The tear drop petrol tank, purple and shining,
A good-looking exterior out to her on loan

On the contempt of the crowd, a silver lining
Which jealousy always has, she is their equal
Her man loves her, and she's not resigning.

"Don't look back, our love must have its sequel
For the mob at my elbow, their dart must be of rue
A destiny will be lost among those dreadful people

Or is it your voice, speaking of the Zoo?
Therefore, my past, I call you! I felt blue
Among the animals, and talked of me and you

But I'm woman! And we nearer, too,
Than animals, to angels. On the bike
I'll survey the scene again, to find clue

Of the only love I know, a human hike
Of arm and shoulder pressing, there! there!
Woman or man, is it love or is it like?"

"This feeling is so strong, what do I care?
Can a man love a woman, is it pat?
Can the universe enter in, do I dare

Put myself into the world, not like a cat
Playing with a ball of wool, but a man
Who finds his half missing, and that

His all he has searched for. If I can
Look into her eyes once more, I'll be sure.
But how the past beckons. If I ran

Straight on to this bike, would I endure
The rat-traps of reason, leave purblind
A world well lost for love. A cure.

I'll jump – reflection makes me blind."
The bike moves. He is left behind.

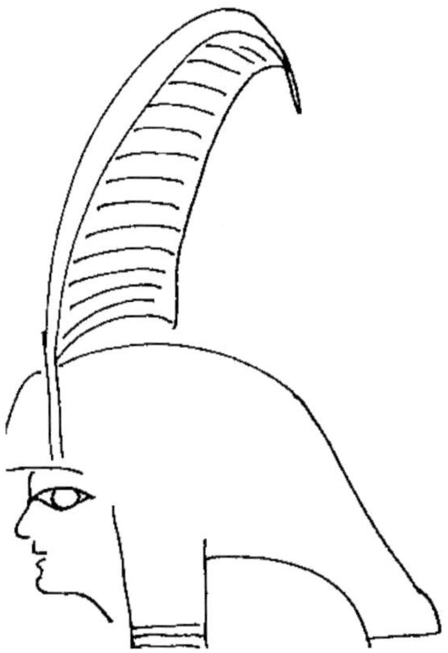

CANTO 13

All progress is based on a universal innate
desire on the part of every organism to
live beyond its income.

Samuel Butler: *Notebooks: 'Life'.*

Catastrophe did not at first strike her.
A sense of missing something far out
As she rode on through the beckoning psyche

Of the morning, and the sun shone out!
Her frail wrist brushed her forehead, she was swept
On with the traffic, and policeman's shout,

And through the lights, she could not have leapt
From her saddle, as with a carnival of noise
She led the traffic for two miles, and wept.

Finally, she hit the kerb, and kept her poise,
As ladies' mags might applaud, by the nearby church
Endured the whistling and the shouts of boys,

And entering in, through the darkened porch,
Saw before the altar, a groom, a bride
Reminding her sharply of her lover in the lurch,

And brushed her tears away. She could not hide
Now, her sense of doom and despair,
A crown of thorns on her head, stitch in her side;

And the space around her like a vanished fair
Where joy had disappeared and the scene
Condensed, in essential and eternal pain -

A transfiguration of what might have been
Became the epitaph of pain and sorrow,
Their living love transformed into a mean

Parody where religion and love borrow
From stuffed reality a foothold on tomorrow.

CANTO 14

I opened to my beloved, but my beloved
had withdrawn himself and was gone:
My soule failed when he spake;
I sought him but could not find him:
I called him, but he gave me no answere.

The Song of Solomon

She was not ready for fate. Back into rain
Now falling, she ran, leapt upon the saddle,
She dithered dangerously in the fast lane,

Then, vroomed to where she had left him to paddle
A lone fisherman, to strain the night's passion,
Where he might be solitary: raddle

His Adonis brow in Grecian fashion?
No sign of him netting daytime's truth,
He wasn't on the pavement, in a session

Of *post coitum* sadness, nor was the youth
Harking at the bus-stop for the beat
In traffic of passing skin and ruth.

He had gone. Her acrobatic feat
Of leaving passenger behind, was a ruse
Of fate, so destiny could clamp the meat

In the trap to accommodate and use
All the chimera since the world began
To eat the fare of romance. Give their views.

Did the pterodactyl foresee the man?
Did the trilobite give a shiver
In the deepest waters, where no light

Can penetrate? Did the protozoa quiver
That one day his mutagenic capacity
Would be lost for love, in a river?

Man-made, by a mortgaged city,
With banks and tower-blocks and railways too,
Did they look forward with reptilian pity,

Or close pitiless eyes to the Zoo
Where her lover had gone, perhaps
Asking the original dumb animals who

Probably were more faithful than the chaps
Bustling around in suits and loving women
Instead of mating yearly, taking naps

All the rest of the time? Who saw her comin'
As she twirled the motor bike down Grafton Street
Dismounting, and pretending to be humming?

Truth was, she felt bitter-sweet
With mood and madness, meaning and moon,
Drunken as a rainbow sorrow on a beat

Of wilful forgetting, her everlasting noon,
Anxiety, that their love was over soon.

CANTO 15

What is honour? A word. What is that word, honour? Air...
'Tis insensible, then. Yea, to the dead.
But will it not live with the living? No.

William Shakespeare *Henry IV*, Part 1 Act V Scene 1

In the recesses of the bar, the mean
And tawdry acolytes of passion sipped
At drinks, took puffs from fags and keen

Inhaling of the fetid air. They dipped
The day's newsprint into the squalor of mind,
Filled with last night's formulae. They kipped

Until the daylight raised the blind
On their anthill bereavements, to sow a scene
Where scorn and impudence can find

Dull fiction. Internecine wars between
Themselves and the shabby suits they wore,
The elbows shining and the pant seats mean.

They looked forward to the core
Of the spectacle, young love being destroyed.
When they saw her, there was a roar.

In the seamy recesses despair was buoyed
On alcoholic bets of poison liquor –
Their dimmer on so hope could be annoyed.

So squander feeling in this ticker
Love, loveless, a ripped and dirty knicker.

CANTO 16

His honour rooted in dishonour stood
And faith unfaithful kept him falsely true.

Alfred Lord Tennyson *Lancelot and Elaine,* 871

It seemed as if the secrets they had shared
Were prised out of the oyster bed of pearl.
He looked at her, too desperately cared.

"You are the first, and the only girl
I have ever loved. And yet you went,
Making me feel I was a foolish churl."

The crowd looked on, amused at his keen vent,
Their boring day transformed into a game.
She knew the conversation should be spent

Somewhere quite else, but so deep her shame,
It drew her into such hauteur, such finick
To deny her love, why it was just the same.

How to explain she must go to the clinic,
For dangerous to love it was, if love they must,
Yet rational planning made her feel a cynic?

And so right there love crumbled into dust
Before the paraphernalia, a wizardry fated
To programme passion, turn it to plotted lust.

How explain she'd been with one she hated
Had wedged herself hopelessly in type,
A granite child of probability, sated

On hunger that was nothing but a hype?
Now, before true love, they felt their loss,
The years behind so empty, how to wipe

Away the tawdry past and so emboss
On their hearts the solemn pledge a monk
Feels in his nightly sacrifice to the cross?

Silence. So he turned to her: "I'm drunk!
You left me, you rode into the sunset,
You didn't show me too much spunk,

But left me, lying on the parapet
Of my broken dreams, where the castle
Crumbled, and you deserted, circumspect.

You left me with my veins open, a passel
Of words to suture live my head
And heart. This almighty hassle –

Life was easier then, in the bed
Of NY heroin, now, *there* was calm,
Cold. For five friends dead

This cold fear, live in Uncle Sam,
A grave watery, and echoing, a feeling
Which manipulates the living in a sham

Advertising of life's extras, like a healing
That came with love. But this death
And five-fold dead!" Here he is, reeling

From pub to alcoholic taxi, where the breath
Of ancient ritual is flayed to a drop
Of cold moisture on the window. Seth

Expiring on the plains of reason, can hop
Over an old grave and a sacred vow
And he sees in nationhood a sop

To people's dreams, rather as the cow
Worshipped in twilight plain could be in youth
Killed by an old man any old how:

To find in drunken embrace, a truth,
A twist of notes in a fingered pocket
Nightmares in taxis, and a sleuth

Host to interesting theories, rocket
Off offending daydream, palatial lusts
Take off, like the eye within its socket

Flies on the unsuitable love object, crusts
Of admiration banquet where the dawn
Chorus sets a poem a-flutter with musts.

Such a youth, a blade of grass in a lawn
Of broken glass. A beautiful form
That yet seeks to break his image, pawn

His soul in sordid sexual encounters. Porn
Queen for a lad, servant for a master,
Whatever your fantasy, he's the norm.

But as they sat on the bench, the castor
Wheels of the drunks' table slid and glided
Now, shaking like reluctant pastor

Whose submission to the divine will elided
Self, ego, ambition, whole lives' aim,
Sheep shorn whom the mob derided,

He bowed his head. Simplicity. The same
Head had lain blissful on her breast,
And in a tender moment breathed her name,

Now asks for severance. The test
That fate so cruelly set has proven
Circumstance would undo lovers, of the best

Calibre, and love itself behoven
To accident, and counting its cost
As if every minute, a separate coven

Of witches brooded on infidelity, and tossed
Indiscretion before the lovers, a tourniquet
Ill-made and bursting heart embossed

For throwing to the mob, an ill-made bouquet
Of faithless flowers, and indiscriminate affection,
Each insulting blossom brought a soubriquet,

But she could only say his name: perfection.
He turned pale, and denied the power of love,
The past too heavy in a predilection

To deny the flight of the dove.
A thorn in his ringless hand, hard to fit.
No challenge to the known. Should she shove

Recent excavated feelings, spit
Out passionate words which now were hollow
Before his personhood? Better split.

Why demean herself and stay? Would she wallow
In entreaties, imploring a second *if.*
Her fault, the motor bike a shallow

Interpreter of space before they had a tiff.
Like a gourd, cut into being, an idea miff.

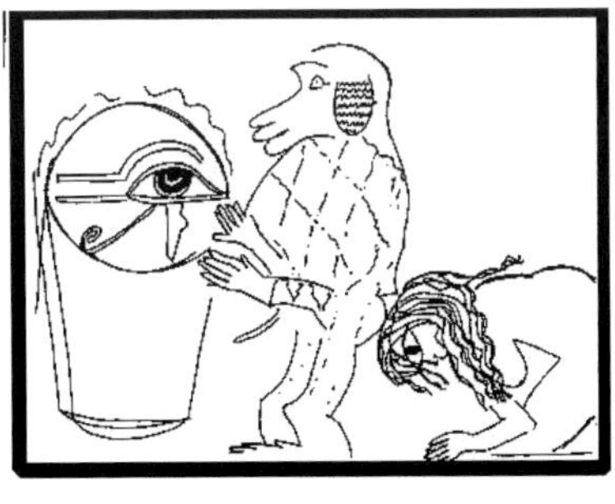

CANTO 17

His flight was madness: when our actions do not
Our fears do make us traitors.

William Shakespeare, *Macbeth* Act IV, Scene 2

The idea of a possible world where peek the given
Into the self, receipted like a quiff
Enfolding the hair, like a cherished leaven

To all imaginings, and desiring lift
To Paradise, but remaining until now
In a seamless garment where no rift

Occurs. But he, in the breaking, would least allow
He has been broken. In that breaking
Now complete, self wrenched away, any how.

Despite the adjusted tears in her aching
Heart, the parting was irrevocable,
Fated, ordained in their forsaking

Of each other. He ran, as if unaccountable
To the door. "If", he shouted, "you felt
Like leaving on your motor bike – understandable!

If the feather in the envelope of your pelt
Weighed against my heart, did not make compact,
If the morning sun crept in and dealt

Me a strange look, do you suspect
Me after my wordless star
Rested in you, inviolate, perfect?

So, you deny the peace that followed, on a par
With the greatest joy I have ever known,
Simply because we were not what we are?

Go then, go then. And betray the grown
Woman in you. You feel so free, so free
Riding away on your bike on loan

From your domestic self. You left me,
Standing bereft like the boy in Hamelin,
Outside the magic mound where children see

Forever the Pied Piper of their rambling
Natures, and dance for charity
Forbidden their futures. Is it worth gambling

For the music of the pipes, posterity
Is music that is revved up,
To throw the same glance backward, for clarity?"

"I heard only the honking of horns. Fed up
With the screeching cacophony, I tried to stop
But was carried forward, nearly threw up

With the stink and fumes, emissions. A cop
Waved to me. Nauseous, I rode on
Feeling like a sorcerer's dancing mop,

Waiting for the magic word to load on
My anxiety, jerk me to a halt.
In the escapade, there was no code on

Which I could rely. Was it my fault
I was new to the bike, quite afraid? –
The makers' instructions needed a pinch
of salt

I'm not an automaton. But the unpaid
Motor bike sent into reverse
Last night, when we two laid

In sweet possibility the tapestry in Erse.
Language made easy. Confident
We could be different, we were not worse

Than those who make public commitment
And behind closed doors carry on charade.
We were the fullness of ourselves, indifferent

To the sweet honeyed tracts of trade
Brandished in magazines in bright illustration –
The surface only, and the smooth tirade.

What matter if I, the soul of a nation,
A frozen out why mark, or connotation?

CANTO 18

The watchmen that went about the citie, found me
they smote me, they wounded me
the keepers of the walles to away my vaile from me

The Song of Solomon

Yet, as she looked askance, at the handsome
Tearful face, she saw a shadow fall.
An aged poet loomed, trying the air to sweeten

With his incongruous shadow, greyer than a pall.
His ashen face with ragged beard looked cursed
He pulled the protesting Adonis to the wall.

Here is a way a she-poet might be worst,
Here was a way her beauty be undone, warp
With feigned love a trembling boy, with pursed

Purple leprous lips give satisfied gawp,
And quieten feeling with a drink of sympathy,
Make hatred like the aftermath of agit-prop

Spike the young forms verging on fertility.
Flowers in summer hurt him, he could coup
A prodigal nature he hated so to see.

Glad that the worst was happening, grouped
Outside, three women kept up appearance, a taxi
Ticked over for a ride on poetry, the muse pooped

For the night of the flesh carnival. A waxy
Effigy, their common hatred of excellence.
Their doll, to prick the pride of this doxy

Lest she bloom, have a lovely efflorescence,
Become a poet of note and lasting fame,
– Jealous of the beauty of transcendence;

While he, with five friends dead, was lame,
Like the boy in Hamelin, and quite unaware
His destruction of himself held no shame.

For life for him had never been very fair.
He lay still at the barque of his dark Odyssey
The old grey bard knew how to tap young despair

And on the polluted waters of life, he was free
To embrace with drunken arm the wilted shoulder
Support him to the taxi. The three women's glee

At a young girl poet defeated in love was colder
Than the embrace of death. Dare be dream Queen
A crowd of three or four is always bolder

And the old bard, mocking, sang "Dark Rosaleen"
That Spanish ale would give her hope
(while he could have the boy for self-esteem).

The magic incantatory song became soap
Opera with his traditional martyr's whinge
Which sneered at her efforts to cope

Now that the magic love undid the hinge
On respectable behaviour, a patriot's proband
Flourished in the drinking and the binge

Of sentiment and violence, that was love of land.
The girl, flayed whole in her alcove
Was debased, as she saw the bard's wandering hand

Insult her lover with caress of mauve
Suggestion, and away they drove.

CANTO 19

I charge you, O daughters of Jerusalem,
If you find my beloved,
That you will tell him I am sick of love.

The Song of Solomon

His last shout: "Witch! Go exchange
Reality for dreams. Just get my message:
In my pocket there is the loose change

Of the decade's debate, and love's suffrage.
I'll go down to the quays to find a new
Love, here there is no refuge."

He clasped a whiskey bottle, scarf askew
Peered out of the taxi. Stained glass
Shimmered as the smoke withdrew

And the fresh air let her pass
Invited guest to the evening's beauty,
The skies of Dublin like the robes at Mass,

When the priest falls in awe and piety
Before the transubstantive host, and prays
For himself and the world, a duty

Felt keenly by the worshippers. Her love pays
Now, on the profane sacrilege of youth.
He pulls his red scarf, and he lays

Two fingers on his cheek – no ruth.
"Witch!" He stamps his foot, a mundane
Goodbye to years, greets varnished truth.

She sees him go between the hulls of pain
Darkness her face, and she can't believe
What's happened. Plays the reel again.

But he's gone, and she goes home to grieve
Falling asleep on the divan bed
A tree in Spring that refused the leaf.

Morning comes like the silver head
Of a stranger probing strange fears,
She jerks awake, goes over what he's said.

She can find no relief, not even in tears,
Pulls on her clothes. The bike is parked
In the pub yard. She goes back amid leers

And jeers from men who feel marked,
Who sip a hair of the dog, full of venom
That destiny has left others unmarked,

Squalor and bad accounts of women!
They stare while she beseeches the bar
Was he really here? The love of my bosom?

She feels naked, like a vivid scar
In a young face, with promises life will mar.

CANTO 20

Quai fossi attraversati o quai catene
trovasti, per che del passare innanzi
dovessite cosi spogliar la spene

Dante *Purgatorio XXXI*

How keep the faith? The years a crescent
Moon that awaits like the first hope
A light before the abyss, before its descent.

So, what is real? She doesn't know how to cope
Joins a rock band, the first girl drummer
And spins a fantasy of human life; a dope

Of revolution, Abraxus, and the mummer
Of each false pendulum swing into barbarism –
Making love a recreation – what a bummer!

I can no longer break myself, a prison
Of truth, beneath your wheel of life,
I can no longer give myself a schism

Between truth and lie, and be a wife
And widow to the shadow of your promise –
I can no longer run in the streets, rife

With the false truth of the mob, be remiss
To my own true self, and to the tears,
I can no longer love without the premise

That I need you too. The river weirs
Are lapping with the footsteps of the holy
While I spendthrift time, with seers

Who are corrupt as idols, are wholly
Given to pleasing, who smile when gold
Is panned before them. I, solely,

Plant my graveyard and yours. Bold
With the stench of decaying lilies
I crumble the yellow sepal, who told

You I love you? Not I. The endless tillies
Pouring out, out of the milk churn at night
Change into nightmare horses, into fillies

Who canter forever to fill the blight
Of time and space, the black void
Where tenderness is off-duty, where the right

To be loved may never happen. Best to avoid
All chance, hope. To rest undetermined,
Resist to the end, undo Freud,

Throw to the raincoat brigade, in vermined
Cinemas for society's bashes,
Aspirations for lips carmined

For destiny, who will not be outdone. Lashes
Of fate on sale, a cat o' nine tails –
Who looks on lovers after car crashes?

Here in the pub, of Lilliputian scale
Sordid limp lives, just going out
On the decade of synchronicity. A wall-wail

And a last curse (of minor doubt):
Reason quenches love, when love's a sin.
Honour, dimmed through the centuries, gives a shout

In the streets, just as if skin
Were the gateway of trust. But it's a word,
A name, how undo the curse, free her to win

For a short time again that quiet bird
Of peace, between breast and breast, like a flower?
How come their time was short, more like a surd

A mathematical impossibility only. The loan
On her spirit increased its weight
So she waxed thin, forgot her koan

And the whole future was a skate-
Board over the cliff. Her hair
Fell out in handfuls, for her mate

Had disappeared, and she went to her lair,
A hut in the bottom of the garden.
Each night she prayed the curse into a prayer

And prayed with mind and books and body's burden
To shrivel the noose of a dark devising,
And through her tears she begged pardon

Of every show of love, and revising
Her look at herself, she took some matches
To set fire to the words, that were the baptising

Into being the mood of good, and swatches
Through which the hum of love had sounded
She burned her notebooks, sang songs in snatches.

She spurned philosophy; which her heart confounded
With her disjunctured brain, all were set aflame,
The hopes in beauty that tormented her, rounded

With the one poet who loved, who would tame
Curiosity like a lamp a moth,
Dictionaries that would largely take the blame

For confusing divination, and the behemoth:
The web of reality, spun and discarded
Into the tired shells of words, the aftermath

Of exploded experience were like dreams carded
Into notebooks, and were tossed upon the blaze –
Thus did I dream my nights, Osiris. Recorded

Painstakingly in the tenebrae of days
Without you, soggy remnants of city lighting
And spectral shadows your eyes, your death stays

Even lonelier through our in-fighting.
The half-developed structures in my jotters
Pin you into wholeness on my sighting.

Now, in flames, you are one with the blotters
Of history, who wipe out legend with rationale
And leave us cultural desert, dirty rotters!

In this hot blaze my soul unites with you, special
Marriage of the contingent, that met the poets' ban –
Take heed, flames, we are one! Who will cavil

Now that cohesion has this plan!
Our formless foolishness will once more perish
Into a perfect shape that loves to scan,

This genius of mine a dervish
Dance of the timeless brain, so burn away
Those who thought our love they would ravish

A cinder trace will form another day,
A banished love the secret and the mystery,
And they will never find another way

In which our private moments make up history.
If they invade like leprous germs our passion
They cannot destroy what is our own consistory,

And if they try to decipher in their fashion
Our secret wording locked into our clay
A hieroglyphic conundrum is their ration!

Why did she not with him stay?
Why did she go on the highway with her bike?
Across the Styx I'll take you one fine day

And no remorse attend our pyre. To like
Romance impossible, now he was a goner;
There was nothing left – no little tyche

Some months hence to be born. To the end a loner,
She tossed on the flame the flower of honour.

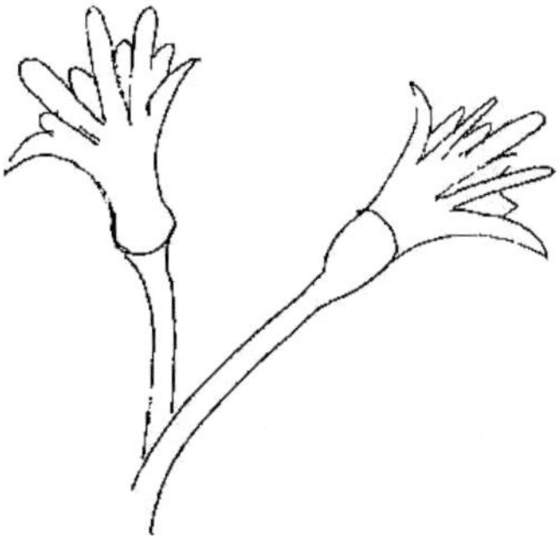

Acknowledgements

Thanks are due to the editors of *Temenos,* London, and *Temenos Academy Review* and in particular to the late Kathleen Raine, in whose journal *Temenos 12* an extract from this work (Canto 4) appeared in 1991.